HOCKEY JOURNAL

PERSONAL STATS TRACKER

Date: _____

Hockey League Level: _____

Location: _____

Team Name: _____

Opponent: _____

Position: _____

Shots Taken: _____   Goals: _____

Assists: _____   Power Play Goals: _____

Short Handed Goals: _____   Overtime Goals: _____

Game Winning Goal (Y/N): _____

Penalties: _____

Penalty Minutes: _____

Favorite Game Memory: _____
_____

Additional Game Notes/Stats:
_____
_____
_____
_____
_____
_____
_____

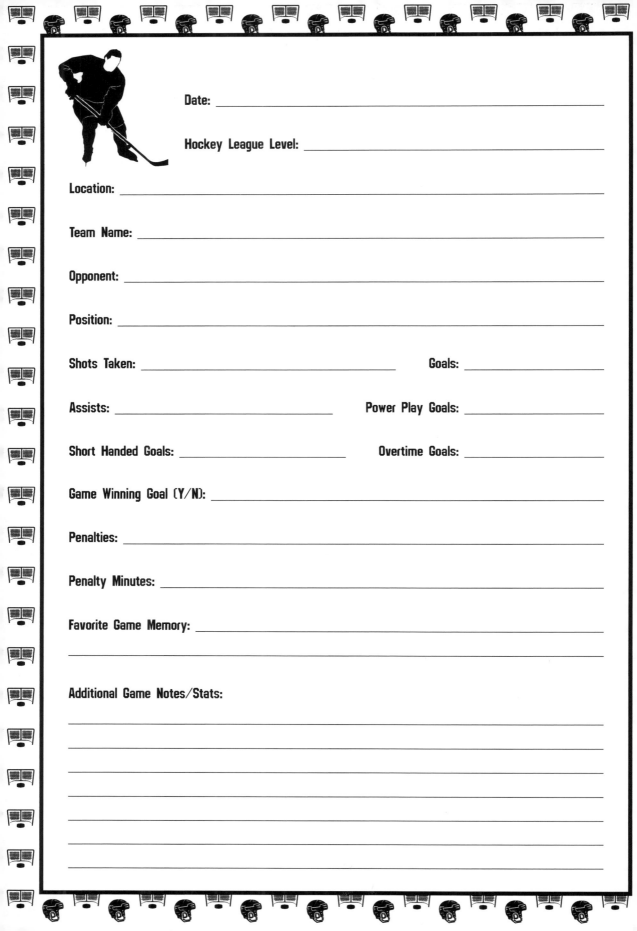

Date: _____

Hockey League Level: _____

Location: _____

Team Name: _____

Opponent: _____

Position: _____

Shots Taken: _____ Goals: _____

Assists: _____ Power Play Goals: _____

Short Handed Goals: _____ Overtime Goals: _____

Game Winning Goal (Y/N): _____

Penalties: _____

Penalty Minutes: _____

Favorite Game Memory: _____
_____

Additional Game Notes/Stats:
_____
_____
_____
_____
_____
_____
_____
_____

Date: _____

Hockey League Level: _____

Location: _____

Team Name: _____

Opponent: _____

Position: _____

Shots Taken: _____   Goals: _____

Assists: _____   Power Play Goals: _____

Short Handed Goals: _____   Overtime Goals: _____

Game Winning Goal (Y/N): _____

Penalties: _____

Penalty Minutes: _____

Favorite Game Memory: _____

_____

Additional Game Notes/Stats:

_____

_____

_____

_____

_____

_____

_____

Date: _____

Hockey League Level: _____

Location: _____

Team Name: _____

Opponent: _____

Position: _____

Shots Taken: _____   Goals: _____

Assists: _____   Power Play Goals: _____

Short Handed Goals: _____   Overtime Goals: _____

Game Winning Goal (Y/N): _____

Penalties: _____

Penalty Minutes: _____

Favorite Game Memory: _____
_____

Additional Game Notes/Stats:
_____
_____
_____
_____
_____
_____
_____
_____

Date: _____

Hockey League Level: _____

Location: _____

Team Name: _____

Opponent: _____

Position: _____

Shots Taken: _____ Goals: _____

Assists: _____ Power Play Goals: _____

Short Handed Goals: _____ Overtime Goals: _____

Game Winning Goal (Y/N): _____

Penalties: _____

Penalty Minutes: _____

Favorite Game Memory: _____
_____

Additional Game Notes/Stats:
_____
_____
_____
_____
_____
_____
_____
_____

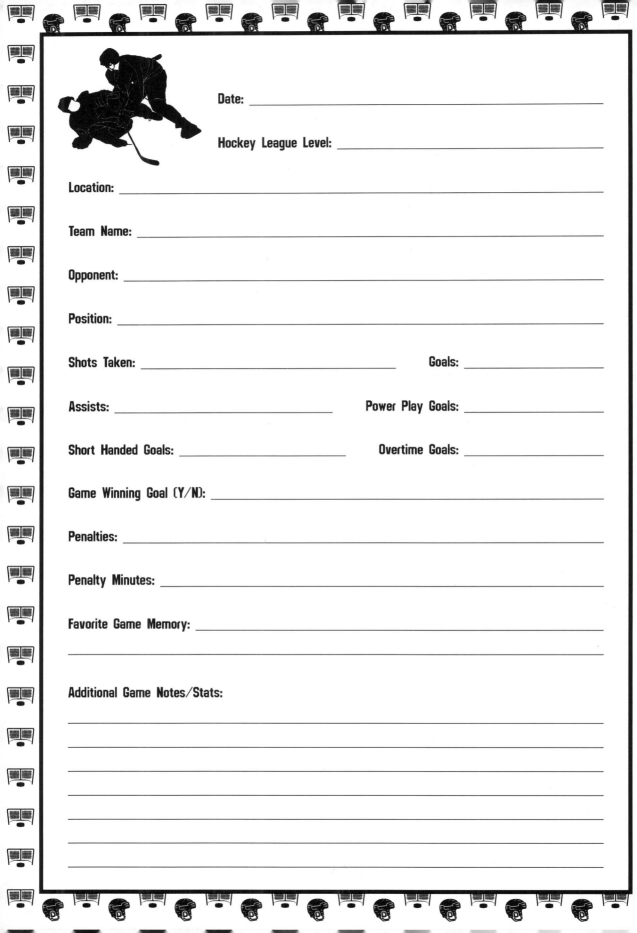

Date: _____

Hockey League Level: _____

Location: _____

Team Name: _____

Opponent: _____

Position: _____

Shots Taken: _____   Goals: _____

Assists: _____   Power Play Goals: _____

Short Handed Goals: _____   Overtime Goals: _____

Game Winning Goal (Y/N): _____

Penalties: _____

Penalty Minutes: _____

Favorite Game Memory: _____
_____

Additional Game Notes/Stats:
_____
_____
_____
_____
_____
_____
_____
_____

Date: _____

Hockey League Level: _____

Location: _____

Team Name: _____

Opponent: _____

Position: _____

Shots Taken: _____   Goals: _____

Assists: _____   Power Play Goals: _____

Short Handed Goals: _____   Overtime Goals: _____

Game Winning Goal (Y/N): _____

Penalties: _____

Penalty Minutes: _____

Favorite Game Memory: _____

_____

Additional Game Notes/Stats:

_____

_____

_____

_____

_____

_____

_____

_____

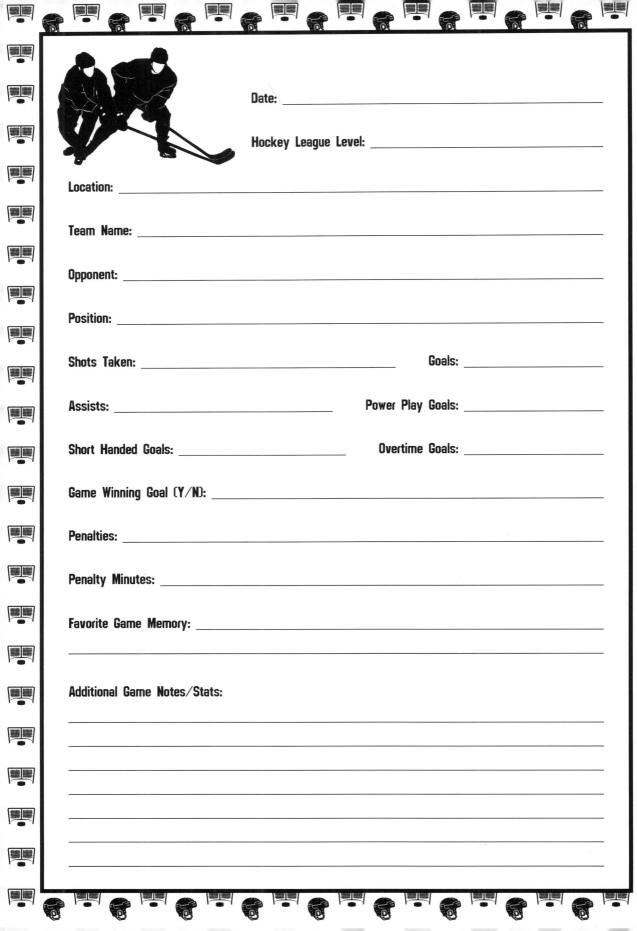

Date: _____

Hockey League Level: _____

Location: _____

Team Name: _____

Opponent: _____

Position: _____

Shots Taken: _____   Goals: _____

Assists: _____   Power Play Goals: _____

Short Handed Goals: _____   Overtime Goals: _____

Game Winning Goal (Y/N): _____

Penalties: _____

Penalty Minutes: _____

Favorite Game Memory: _____
_____

Additional Game Notes/Stats:

_____
_____
_____
_____
_____
_____
_____

Date: _____

Hockey League Level: _____

Location: _____

Team Name: _____

Opponent: _____

Position: _____

Shots Taken: _____ Goals: _____

Assists: _____ Power Play Goals: _____

Short Handed Goals: _____ Overtime Goals: _____

Game Winning Goal (Y/N): _____

Penalties: _____

Penalty Minutes: _____

Favorite Game Memory: _____

_____

Additional Game Notes/Stats:

_____

_____

_____

_____

_____

_____

_____

_____

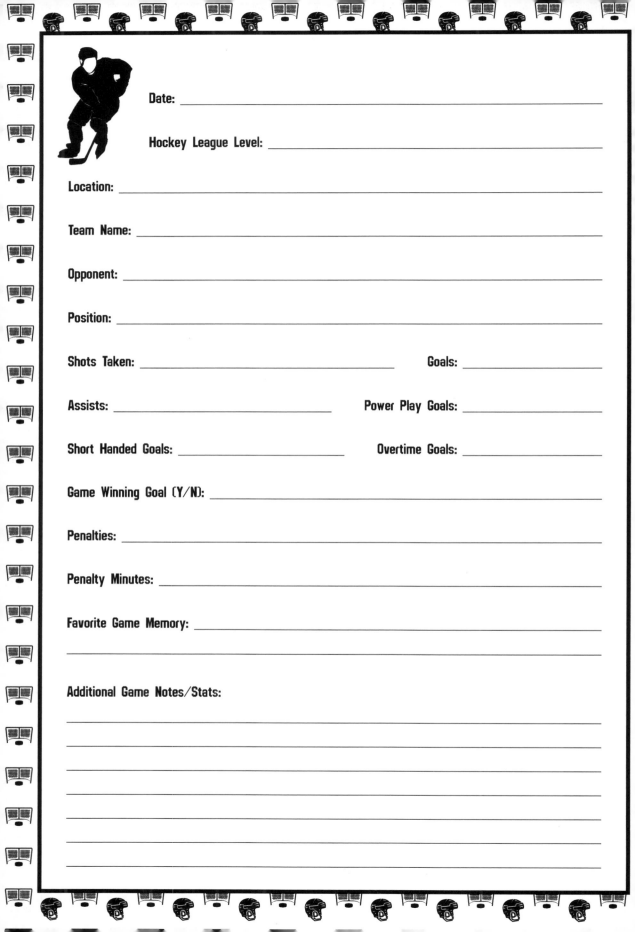

Date: _____

Hockey League Level: _____

Location: _____

Team Name: _____

Opponent: _____

Position: _____

Shots Taken: _____   Goals: _____

Assists: _____   Power Play Goals: _____

Short Handed Goals: _____   Overtime Goals: _____

Game Winning Goal (Y/N): _____

Penalties: _____

Penalty Minutes: _____

Favorite Game Memory: _____
_____

Additional Game Notes/Stats:
_____
_____
_____
_____
_____
_____
_____
_____
_____

Date: _____

Hockey League Level: _____

Location: _____

Team Name: _____

Opponent: _____

Position: _____

Shots Taken: _____ Goals: _____

Assists: _____ Power Play Goals: _____

Short Handed Goals: _____ Overtime Goals: _____

Game Winning Goal (Y/N): _____

Penalties: _____

Penalty Minutes: _____

Favorite Game Memory: _____

_____

Additional Game Notes/Stats:

_____

_____

_____

_____

_____

_____

_____

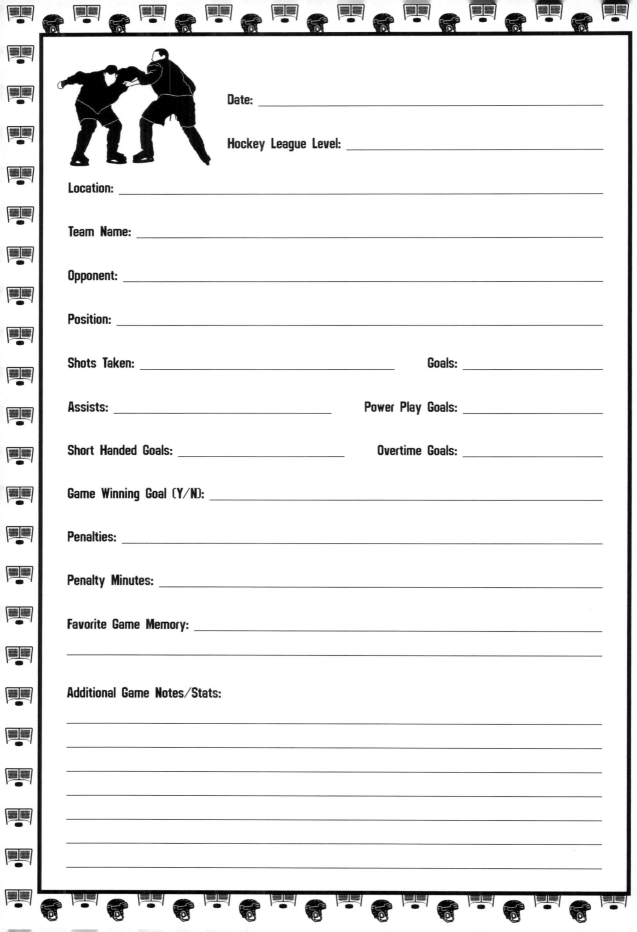

Date: _____

Hockey League Level: _____

Location: _____

Team Name: _____

Opponent: _____

Position: _____

Shots Taken: _____   Goals: _____

Assists: _____   Power Play Goals: _____

Short Handed Goals: _____   Overtime Goals: _____

Game Winning Goal (Y/N): _____

Penalties: _____

Penalty Minutes: _____

Favorite Game Memory: _____
_____

Additional Game Notes/Stats:
_____
_____
_____
_____
_____
_____
_____
_____

Date: _____

Hockey League Level: _____

Location: _____

Team Name: _____

Opponent: _____

Position: _____

Shots Taken: _____   Goals: _____

Assists: _____   Power Play Goals: _____

Short Handed Goals: _____   Overtime Goals: _____

Game Winning Goal (Y/N): _____

Penalties: _____

Penalty Minutes: _____

Favorite Game Memory: _____
_____

Additional Game Notes/Stats:
_____
_____
_____
_____
_____
_____
_____
_____

Date: _____

Hockey League Level: _____

Location: _____

Team Name: _____

Opponent: _____

Position: _____

Shots Taken: _____ Goals: _____

Assists: _____ Power Play Goals: _____

Short Handed Goals: _____ Overtime Goals: _____

Game Winning Goal (Y/N): _____

Penalties: _____

Penalty Minutes: _____

Favorite Game Memory: _____

_____

Additional Game Notes/Stats:

_____

_____

_____

_____

_____

_____

_____

_____

Date: _____

Hockey League Level: _____

Location: _____

Team Name: _____

Opponent: _____

Position: _____

Shots Taken: _____ Goals: _____

Assists: _____ Power Play Goals: _____

Short Handed Goals: _____ Overtime Goals: _____

Game Winning Goal (Y/N): _____

Penalties: _____

Penalty Minutes: _____

Favorite Game Memory: _____
_____

Additional Game Notes/Stats:
_____
_____
_____
_____
_____
_____
_____
_____

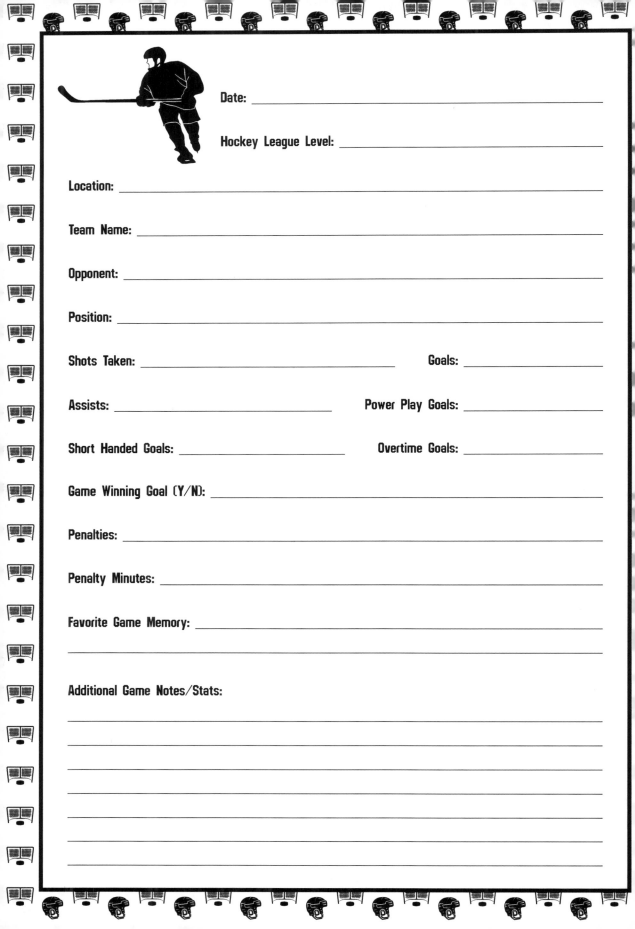

Date: _____

Hockey League Level: _____

Location: _____

Team Name: _____

Opponent: _____

Position: _____

Shots Taken: _____ Goals: _____

Assists: _____ Power Play Goals: _____

Short Handed Goals: _____ Overtime Goals: _____

Game Winning Goal (Y/N): _____

Penalties: _____

Penalty Minutes: _____

Favorite Game Memory: _____

_____

Additional Game Notes/Stats:

_____

_____

_____

_____

_____

_____

_____

Date: _____

Hockey League Level: _____

Location: _____

Team Name: _____

Opponent: _____

Position: _____

Shots Taken: _____ Goals: _____

Assists: _____ Power Play Goals: _____

Short Handed Goals: _____ Overtime Goals: _____

Game Winning Goal (Y/N): _____

Penalties: _____

Penalty Minutes: _____

Favorite Game Memory: _____
_____

Additional Game Notes/Stats:
_____
_____
_____
_____
_____
_____
_____

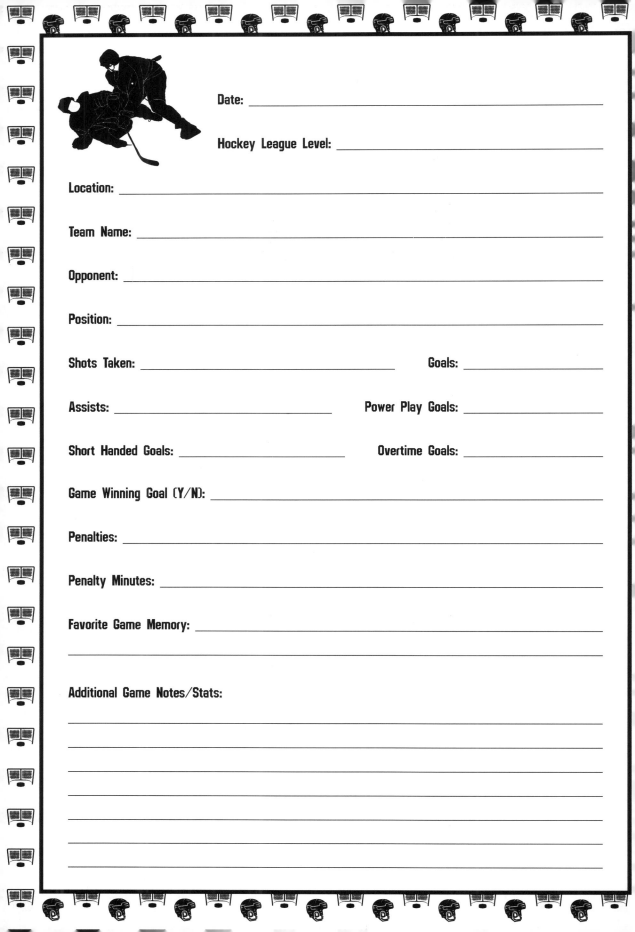

Date: _____

Hockey League Level: _____

Location: _____

Team Name: _____

Opponent: _____

Position: _____

Shots Taken: _____ Goals: _____

Assists: _____ Power Play Goals: _____

Short Handed Goals: _____ Overtime Goals: _____

Game Winning Goal (Y/N): _____

Penalties: _____

Penalty Minutes: _____

Favorite Game Memory: _____

_____

Additional Game Notes/Stats:

_____

_____

_____

_____

_____

_____

_____

Date: _____

Hockey League Level: _____

Location: _____

Team Name: _____

Opponent: _____

Position: _____

Shots Taken: _____   Goals: _____

Assists: _____   Power Play Goals: _____

Short Handed Goals: _____   Overtime Goals: _____

Game Winning Goal (Y/N): _____

Penalties: _____

Penalty Minutes: _____

Favorite Game Memory: _____

_____

Additional Game Notes/Stats:

_____

_____

_____

_____

_____

_____

_____

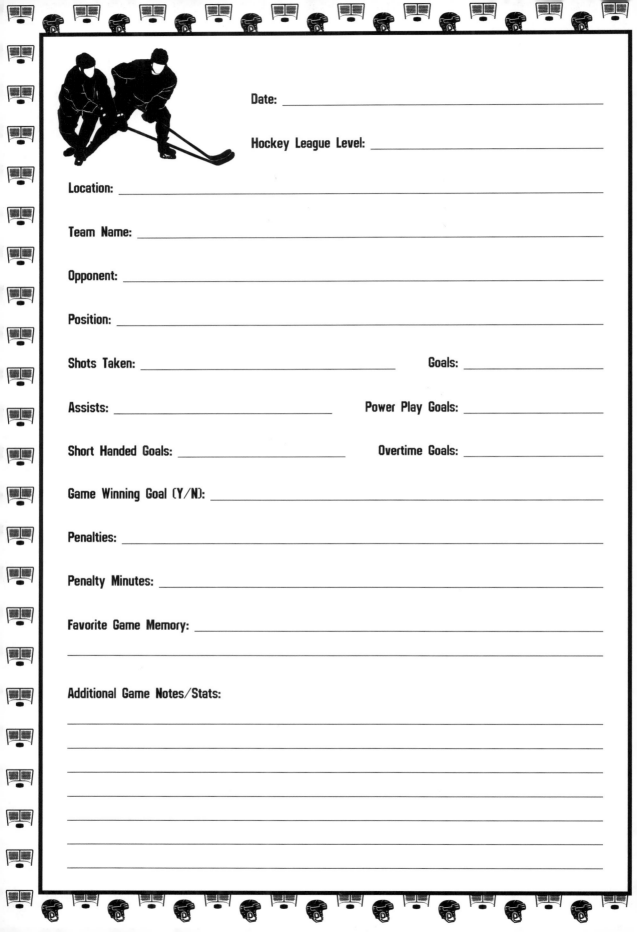

Date: _____

Hockey League Level: _____

Location: _____

Team Name: _____

Opponent: _____

Position: _____

Shots Taken: _____ Goals: _____

Assists: _____ Power Play Goals: _____

Short Handed Goals: _____ Overtime Goals: _____

Game Winning Goal (Y/N): _____

Penalties: _____

Penalty Minutes: _____

Favorite Game Memory: _____

_____

Additional Game Notes/Stats:

_____

_____

_____

_____

_____

_____

_____

_____

Date: _____

Hockey League Level: _____

Location: _____

Team Name: _____

Opponent: _____

Position: _____

Shots Taken: _____ Goals: _____

Assists: _____ Power Play Goals: _____

Short Handed Goals: _____ Overtime Goals: _____

Game Winning Goal (Y/N): _____

Penalties: _____

Penalty Minutes: _____

Favorite Game Memory: _____
_____

Additional Game Notes/Stats:
_____
_____
_____
_____
_____
_____
_____
_____

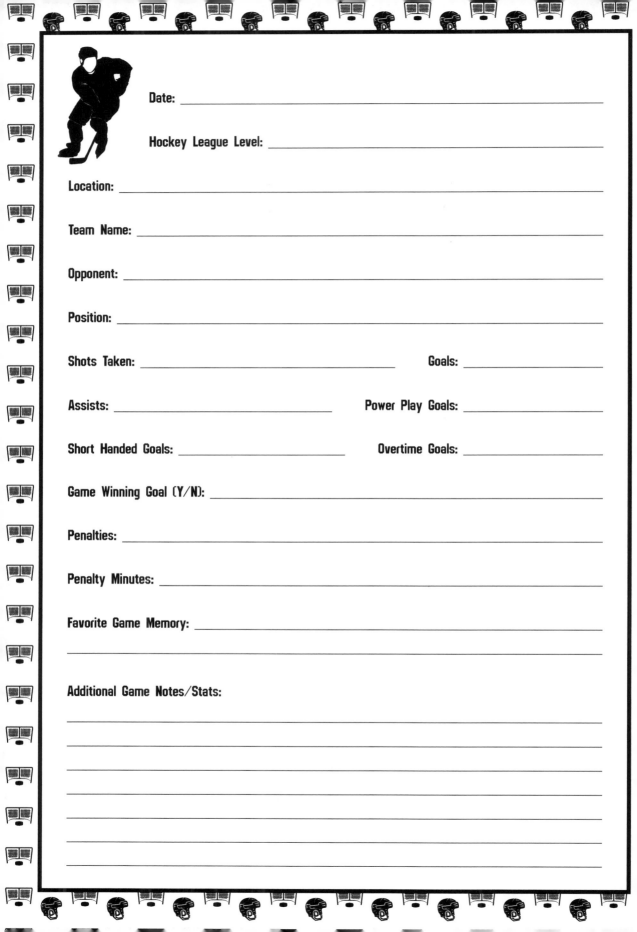

Date: _____

Hockey League Level: _____

Location: _____

Team Name: _____

Opponent: _____

Position: _____

Shots Taken: _____ Goals: _____

Assists: _____ Power Play Goals: _____

Short Handed Goals: _____ Overtime Goals: _____

Game Winning Goal (Y/N): _____

Penalties: _____

Penalty Minutes: _____

Favorite Game Memory: _____
_____

Additional Game Notes/Stats:

_____
_____
_____
_____
_____
_____
_____
_____
_____

Date: _____

Hockey League Level: _____

Location: _____

Team Name: _____

Opponent: _____

Position: _____

Shots Taken: _____   Goals: _____

Assists: _____   Power Play Goals: _____

Short Handed Goals: _____   Overtime Goals: _____

Game Winning Goal (Y/N): _____

Penalties: _____

Penalty Minutes: _____

Favorite Game Memory: _____
_____

Additional Game Notes/Stats:
_____
_____
_____
_____
_____
_____
_____
_____

Date: _____

Hockey League Level: _____

Location: _____

Team Name: _____

Opponent: _____

Position: _____

Shots Taken: _____   Goals: _____

Assists: _____   Power Play Goals: _____

Short Handed Goals: _____   Overtime Goals: _____

Game Winning Goal (Y/N): _____

Penalties: _____

Penalty Minutes: _____

Favorite Game Memory: _____

_____

Additional Game Notes/Stats:

_____

_____

_____

_____

_____

_____

_____

Date: _____

Hockey League Level: _____

Location: _____

Team Name: _____

Opponent: _____

Position: _____

Shots Taken: _____   Goals: _____

Assists: _____   Power Play Goals: _____

Short Handed Goals: _____   Overtime Goals: _____

Game Winning Goal (Y/N): _____

Penalties: _____

Penalty Minutes: _____

Favorite Game Memory: _____

_____

Additional Game Notes/Stats:

_____

_____

_____

_____

_____

_____

_____

_____

Date: _____

Hockey League Level: _____

Location: _____

Team Name: _____

Opponent: _____

Position: _____

Shots Taken: _____   Goals: _____

Assists: _____   Power Play Goals: _____

Short Handed Goals: _____   Overtime Goals: _____

Game Winning Goal (Y/N): _____

Penalties: _____

Penalty Minutes: _____

Favorite Game Memory: _____

_____

Additional Game Notes/Stats:

_____

_____

_____

_____

_____

_____

_____

_____

Date: _____

Hockey League Level: _____

Location: _____

Team Name: _____

Opponent: _____

Position: _____

Shots Taken: _____   Goals: _____

Assists: _____   Power Play Goals: _____

Short Handed Goals: _____   Overtime Goals: _____

Game Winning Goal (Y/N): _____

Penalties: _____

Penalty Minutes: _____

Favorite Game Memory: _____

_____

Additional Game Notes/Stats:

_____

_____

_____

_____

_____

_____

_____

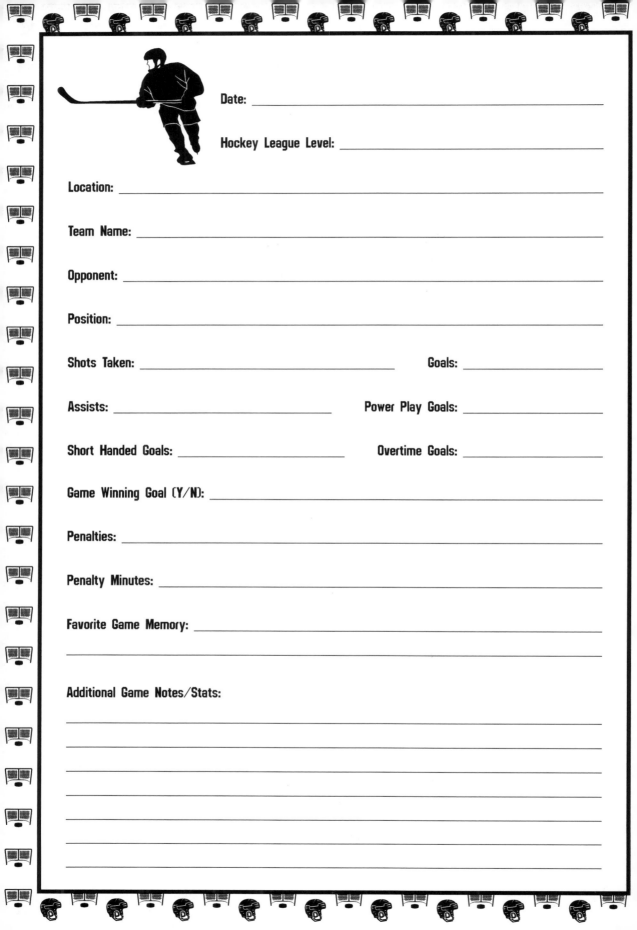

Date: _____

Hockey League Level: _____

Location: _____

Team Name: _____

Opponent: _____

Position: _____

Shots Taken: _____   Goals: _____

Assists: _____   Power Play Goals: _____

Short Handed Goals: _____   Overtime Goals: _____

Game Winning Goal (Y/N): _____

Penalties: _____

Penalty Minutes: _____

Favorite Game Memory: _____

_____

Additional Game Notes/Stats:

_____

_____

_____

_____

_____

_____

_____

Date: _____

Hockey League Level: _____

Location: _____

Team Name: _____

Opponent: _____

Position: _____

Shots Taken: _____ Goals: _____

Assists: _____ Power Play Goals: _____

Short Handed Goals: _____ Overtime Goals: _____

Game Winning Goal (Y/N): _____

Penalties: _____

Penalty Minutes: _____

Favorite Game Memory: _____
_____

Additional Game Notes/Stats:
_____
_____
_____
_____
_____
_____
_____
_____

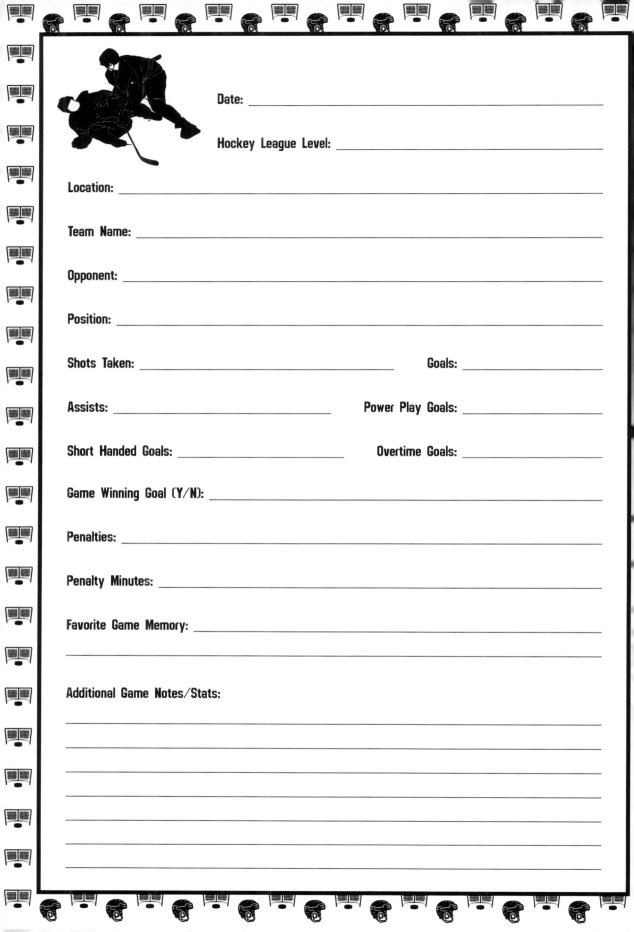

Date: _____

Hockey League Level: _____

Location: _____

Team Name: _____

Opponent: _____

Position: _____

Shots Taken: _____ Goals: _____

Assists: _____ Power Play Goals: _____

Short Handed Goals: _____ Overtime Goals: _____

Game Winning Goal (Y/N): _____

Penalties: _____

Penalty Minutes: _____

Favorite Game Memory: _____

_____

Additional Game Notes/Stats:

_____

_____

_____

_____

_____

_____

_____

_____

Date: _____

Hockey League Level: _____

Location: _____

Team Name: _____

Opponent: _____

Position: _____

Shots Taken: _____   Goals: _____

Assists: _____   Power Play Goals: _____

Short Handed Goals: _____   Overtime Goals: _____

Game Winning Goal (Y/N): _____

Penalties: _____

Penalty Minutes: _____

Favorite Game Memory: _____
_____

Additional Game Notes/Stats:
_____
_____
_____
_____
_____
_____
_____

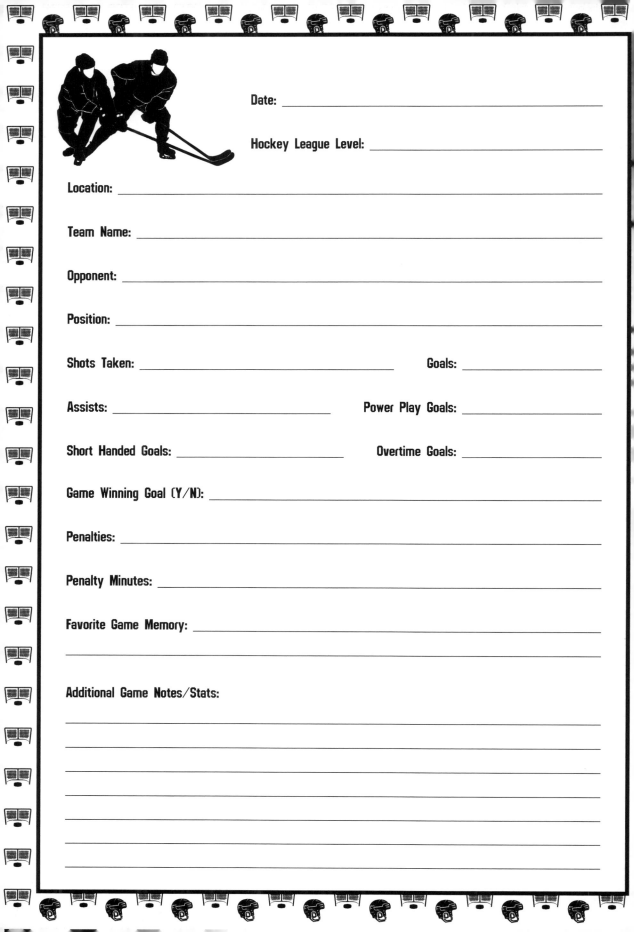

Date: _____

Hockey League Level: _____

Location: _____

Team Name: _____

Opponent: _____

Position: _____

Shots Taken: _____ Goals: _____

Assists: _____ Power Play Goals: _____

Short Handed Goals: _____ Overtime Goals: _____

Game Winning Goal (Y/N): _____

Penalties: _____

Penalty Minutes: _____

Favorite Game Memory: _____

_____

Additional Game Notes/Stats:

_____
_____
_____
_____
_____
_____
_____
_____

Date: _____

Hockey League Level: _____

Location: _____

Team Name: _____

Opponent: _____

Position: _____

Shots Taken: _____ Goals: _____

Assists: _____ Power Play Goals: _____

Short Handed Goals: _____ Overtime Goals: _____

Game Winning Goal (Y/N): _____

Penalties: _____

Penalty Minutes: _____

Favorite Game Memory: _____

_____

Additional Game Notes/Stats:

_____
_____
_____
_____
_____
_____
_____
_____

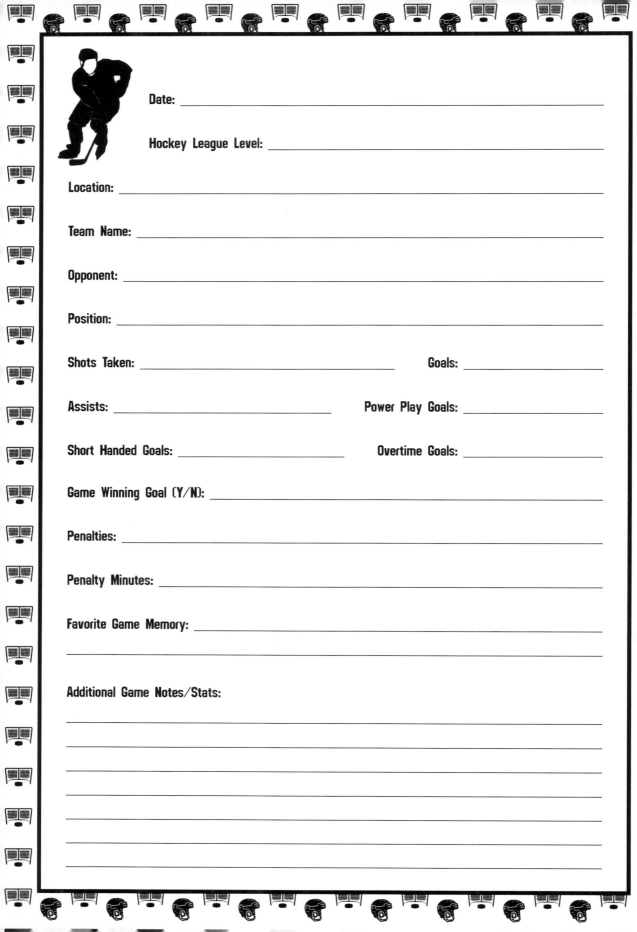

Date: _____

Hockey League Level: _____

Location: _____

Team Name: _____

Opponent: _____

Position: _____

Shots Taken: _____ Goals: _____

Assists: _____ Power Play Goals: _____

Short Handed Goals: _____ Overtime Goals: _____

Game Winning Goal (Y/N): _____

Penalties: _____

Penalty Minutes: _____

Favorite Game Memory: _____
_____

Additional Game Notes/Stats:
_____
_____
_____
_____
_____
_____
_____
_____

Date: _____

Hockey League Level: _____

Location: _____

Team Name: _____

Opponent: _____

Position: _____

Shots Taken: _____ Goals: _____

Assists: _____ Power Play Goals: _____

Short Handed Goals: _____ Overtime Goals: _____

Game Winning Goal (Y/N): _____

Penalties: _____

Penalty Minutes: _____

Favorite Game Memory: _____
_____

Additional Game Notes/Stats:
_____
_____
_____
_____
_____
_____
_____
_____

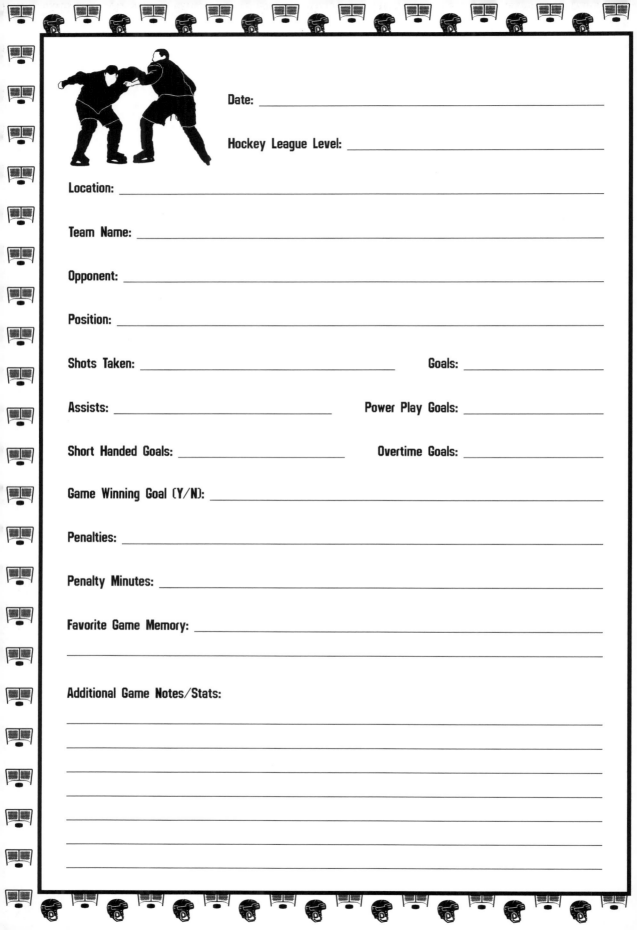

Date: _____

Hockey League Level: _____

Location: _____

Team Name: _____

Opponent: _____

Position: _____

Shots Taken: _____ Goals: _____

Assists: _____ Power Play Goals: _____

Short Handed Goals: _____ Overtime Goals: _____

Game Winning Goal (Y/N): _____

Penalties: _____

Penalty Minutes: _____

Favorite Game Memory: _____
_____

Additional Game Notes/Stats:
_____
_____
_____
_____
_____
_____
_____
_____

Date: _____

Hockey League Level: _____

Location: _____

Team Name: _____

Opponent: _____

Position: _____

Shots Taken: _____   Goals: _____

Assists: _____   Power Play Goals: _____

Short Handed Goals: _____   Overtime Goals: _____

Game Winning Goal (Y/N): _____

Penalties: _____

Penalty Minutes: _____

Favorite Game Memory: _____
_____

Additional Game Notes/Stats:
_____
_____
_____
_____
_____
_____
_____
_____

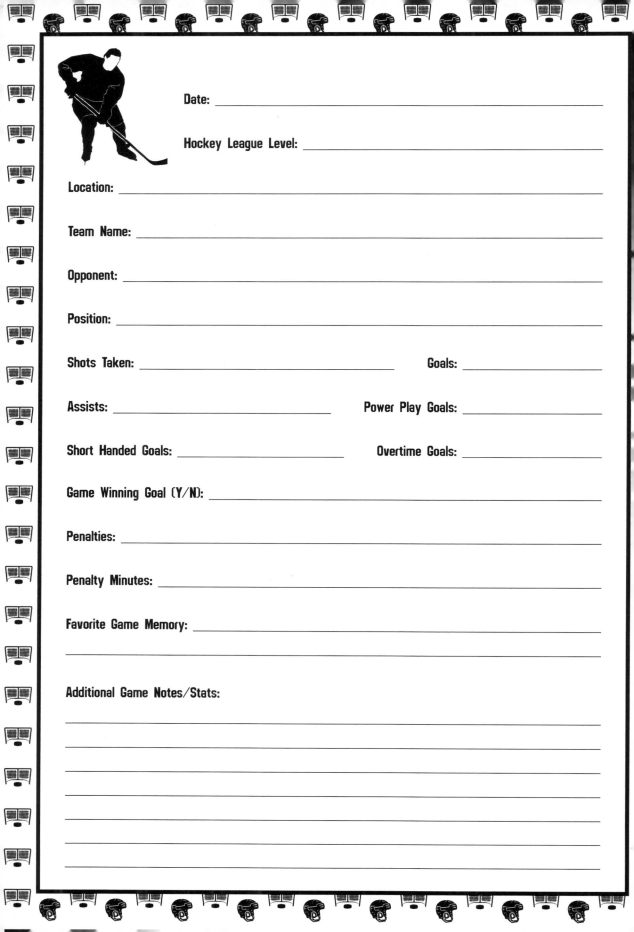

Date: _____

Hockey League Level: _____

Location: _____

Team Name: _____

Opponent: _____

Position: _____

Shots Taken: _____   Goals: _____

Assists: _____   Power Play Goals: _____

Short Handed Goals: _____   Overtime Goals: _____

Game Winning Goal (Y/N): _____

Penalties: _____

Penalty Minutes: _____

Favorite Game Memory: _____

_____

Additional Game Notes/Stats:

_____

_____

_____

_____

_____

_____

_____

_____

Date: _____

Hockey League Level: _____

Location: _____

Team Name: _____

Opponent: _____

Position: _____

Shots Taken: _____ Goals: _____

Assists: _____ Power Play Goals: _____

Short Handed Goals: _____ Overtime Goals: _____

Game Winning Goal (Y/N): _____

Penalties: _____

Penalty Minutes: _____

Favorite Game Memory: _____

_____

Additional Game Notes/Stats:

_____

_____

_____

_____

_____

_____

_____

_____

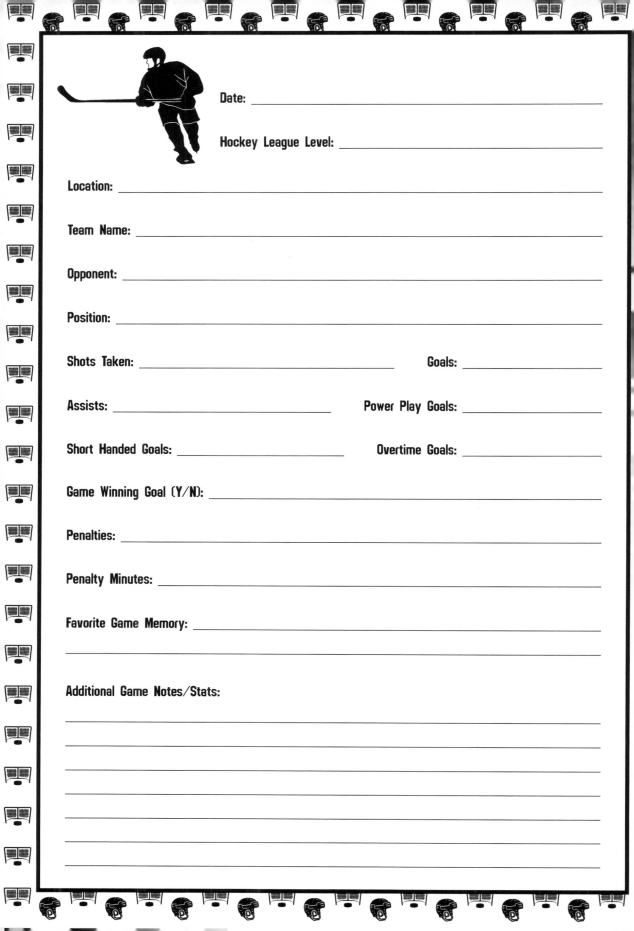

Date: _____

Hockey League Level: _____

Location: _____

Team Name: _____

Opponent: _____

Position: _____

Shots Taken: _____   Goals: _____

Assists: _____   Power Play Goals: _____

Short Handed Goals: _____   Overtime Goals: _____

Game Winning Goal (Y/N): _____

Penalties: _____

Penalty Minutes: _____

Favorite Game Memory: _____
_____

Additional Game Notes/Stats:

_____
_____
_____
_____
_____
_____
_____

Date: _____

Hockey League Level: _____

Location: _____

Team Name: _____

Opponent: _____

Position: _____

Shots Taken: _____ Goals: _____

Assists: _____ Power Play Goals: _____

Short Handed Goals: _____ Overtime Goals: _____

Game Winning Goal (Y/N): _____

Penalties: _____

Penalty Minutes: _____

Favorite Game Memory: _____

_____

Additional Game Notes/Stats:

_____
_____
_____
_____
_____
_____
_____
_____

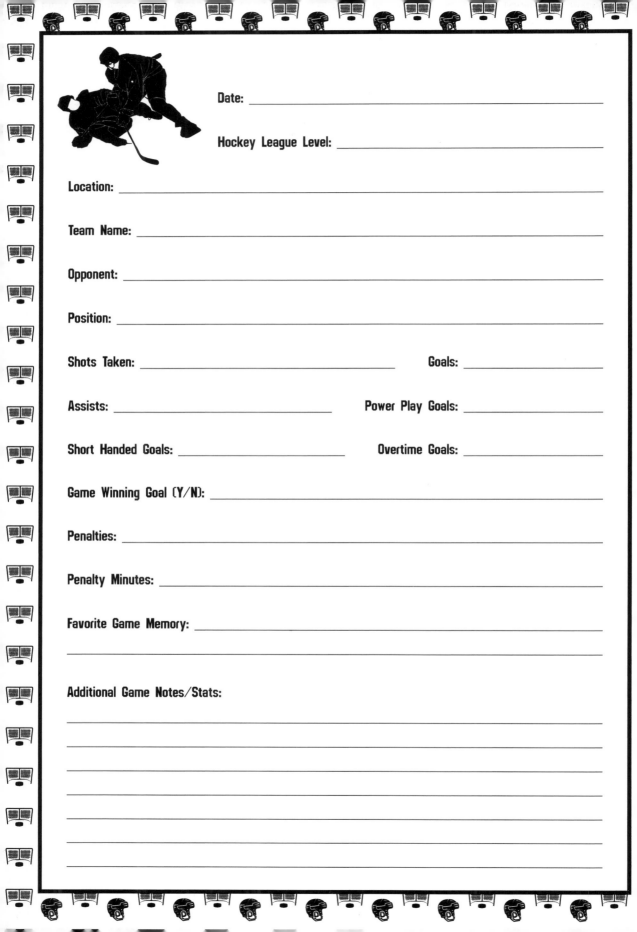

Date: _____

Hockey League Level: _____

Location: _____

Team Name: _____

Opponent: _____

Position: _____

Shots Taken: _____ Goals: _____

Assists: _____ Power Play Goals: _____

Short Handed Goals: _____ Overtime Goals: _____

Game Winning Goal (Y/N): _____

Penalties: _____

Penalty Minutes: _____

Favorite Game Memory: _____

_____

Additional Game Notes/Stats:

_____

_____

_____

_____

_____

_____

_____

Date: _____

Hockey League Level: _____

Location: _____

Team Name: _____

Opponent: _____

Position: _____

Shots Taken: _____   Goals: _____

Assists: _____   Power Play Goals: _____

Short Handed Goals: _____   Overtime Goals: _____

Game Winning Goal (Y/N): _____

Penalties: _____

Penalty Minutes: _____

Favorite Game Memory: _____

_____

Additional Game Notes/Stats:

_____

_____

_____

_____

_____

_____

_____

_____

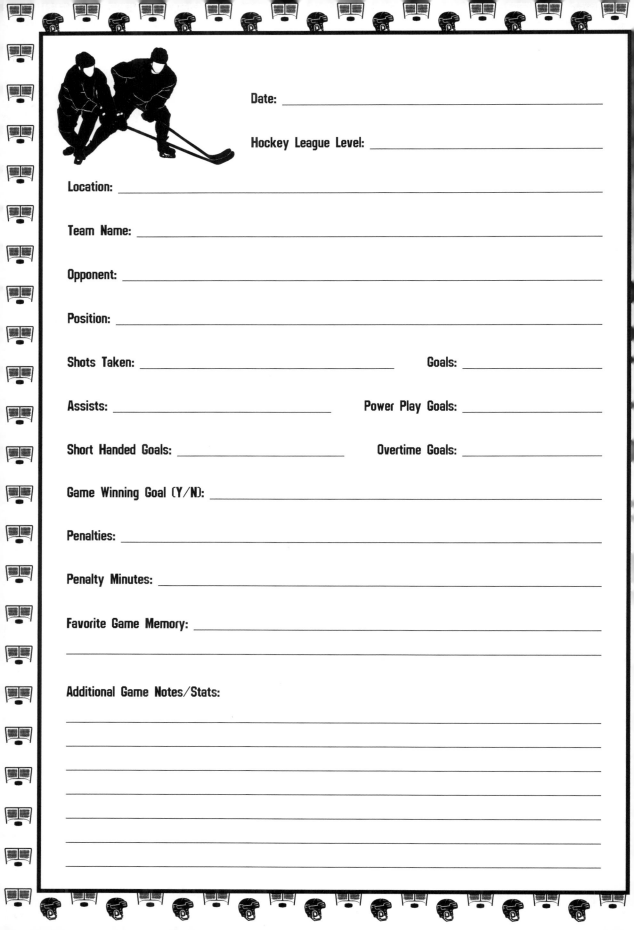

Date: _____

Hockey League Level: _____

Location: _____

Team Name: _____

Opponent: _____

Position: _____

Shots Taken: _____   Goals: _____

Assists: _____   Power Play Goals: _____

Short Handed Goals: _____   Overtime Goals: _____

Game Winning Goal (Y/N): _____

Penalties: _____

Penalty Minutes: _____

Favorite Game Memory: _____
_____

Additional Game Notes/Stats:
_____
_____
_____
_____
_____
_____
_____
_____

Date: _____

Hockey League Level: _____

Location: _____

Team Name: _____

Opponent: _____

Position: _____

Shots Taken: _____ Goals: _____

Assists: _____ Power Play Goals: _____

Short Handed Goals: _____ Overtime Goals: _____

Game Winning Goal (Y/N): _____

Penalties: _____

Penalty Minutes: _____

Favorite Game Memory: _____
_____

Additional Game Notes/Stats:
_____
_____
_____
_____
_____
_____
_____
_____

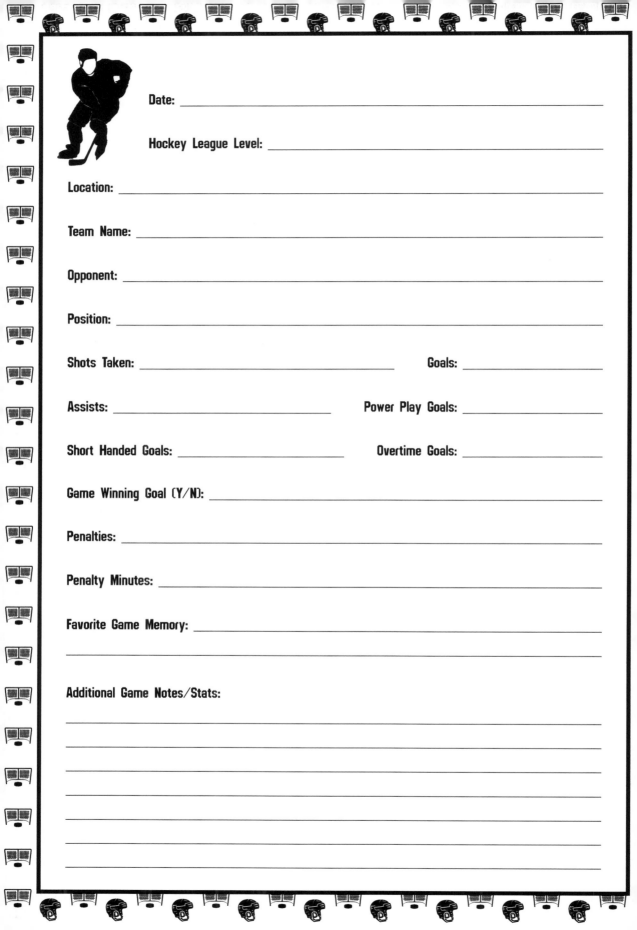

Date: _____

Hockey League Level: _____

Location: _____

Team Name: _____

Opponent: _____

Position: _____

Shots Taken: _____   Goals: _____

Assists: _____   Power Play Goals: _____

Short Handed Goals: _____   Overtime Goals: _____

Game Winning Goal (Y/N): _____

Penalties: _____

Penalty Minutes: _____

Favorite Game Memory: _____

_____

Additional Game Notes/Stats:

_____

_____

_____

_____

_____

_____

_____

Date: _____

Hockey League Level: _____

Location: _____

Team Name: _____

Opponent: _____

Position: _____

Shots Taken: _____   Goals: _____

Assists: _____   Power Play Goals: _____

Short Handed Goals: _____   Overtime Goals: _____

Game Winning Goal (Y/N): _____

Penalties: _____

Penalty Minutes: _____

Favorite Game Memory: _____
_____

Additional Game Notes/Stats:
_____
_____
_____
_____
_____
_____
_____
_____

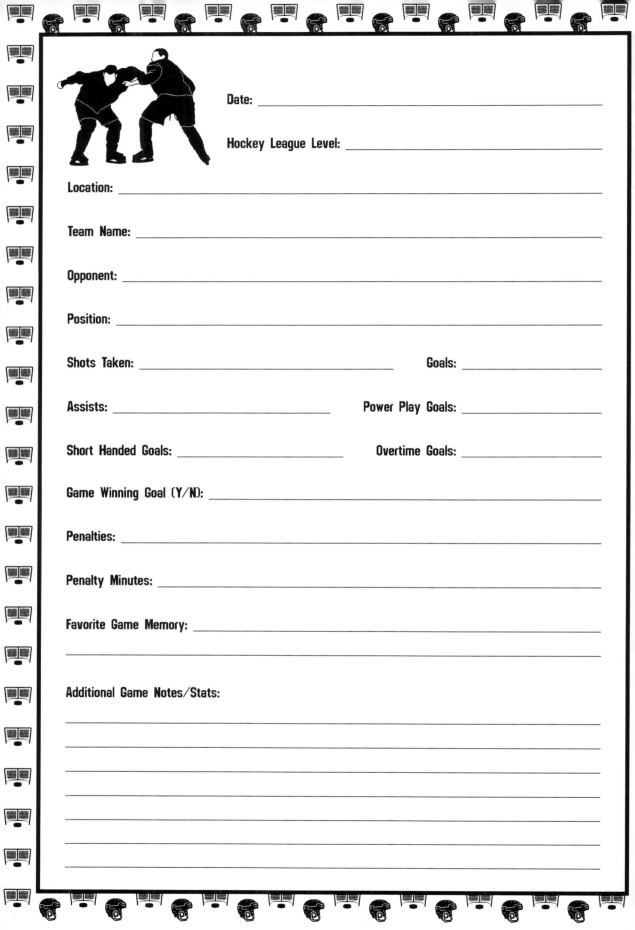

Date: _____

Hockey League Level: _____

Location: _____

Team Name: _____

Opponent: _____

Position: _____

Shots Taken: _____ Goals: _____

Assists: _____ Power Play Goals: _____

Short Handed Goals: _____ Overtime Goals: _____

Game Winning Goal (Y/N): _____

Penalties: _____

Penalty Minutes: _____

Favorite Game Memory: _____

_____

Additional Game Notes/Stats:

_____
_____
_____
_____
_____
_____
_____
_____

Date: _____

Hockey League Level: _____

Location: _____

Team Name: _____

Opponent: _____

Position: _____

Shots Taken: _____   Goals: _____

Assists: _____   Power Play Goals: _____

Short Handed Goals: _____   Overtime Goals: _____

Game Winning Goal (Y/N): _____

Penalties: _____

Penalty Minutes: _____

Favorite Game Memory: _____
_____

Additional Game Notes/Stats:
_____
_____
_____
_____
_____
_____
_____
_____

Date: _____

Hockey League Level: _____

Location: _____

Team Name: _____

Opponent: _____

Position: _____

Shots Taken: _____   Goals: _____

Assists: _____   Power Play Goals: _____

Short Handed Goals: _____   Overtime Goals: _____

Game Winning Goal (Y/N): _____

Penalties: _____

Penalty Minutes: _____

Favorite Game Memory: _____

_____

Additional Game Notes/Stats:

_____
_____
_____
_____
_____
_____
_____
_____

Date: _____

Hockey League Level: _____

Location: _____

Team Name: _____

Opponent: _____

Position: _____

Shots Taken: _____   Goals: _____

Assists: _____   Power Play Goals: _____

Short Handed Goals: _____   Overtime Goals: _____

Game Winning Goal (Y/N): _____

Penalties: _____

Penalty Minutes: _____

Favorite Game Memory: _____
_____

Additional Game Notes/Stats:
_____
_____
_____
_____
_____
_____
_____

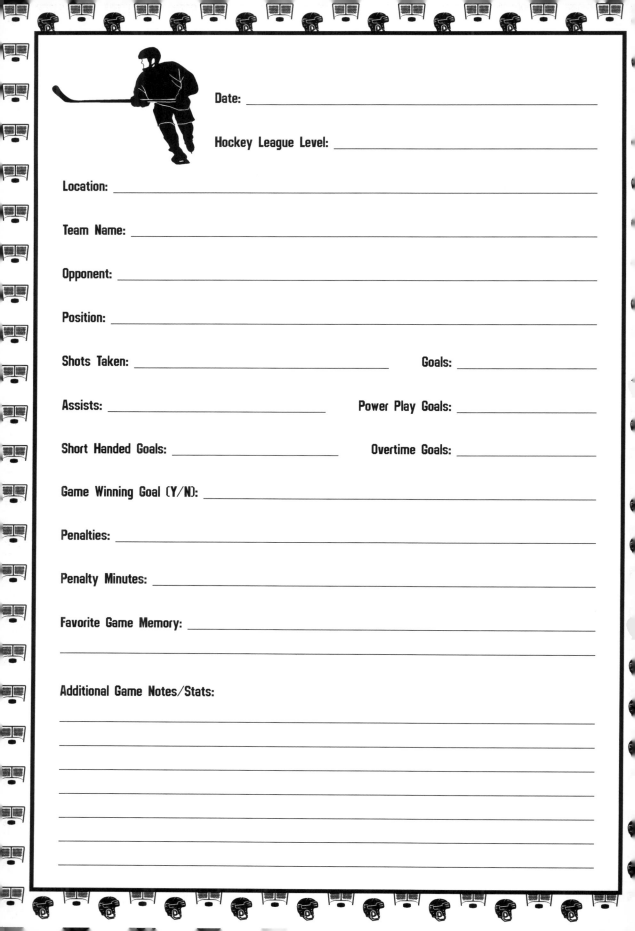

Date: _____

Hockey League Level: _____

Location: _____

Team Name: _____

Opponent: _____

Position: _____

Shots Taken: _____ Goals: _____

Assists: _____ Power Play Goals: _____

Short Handed Goals: _____ Overtime Goals: _____

Game Winning Goal (Y/N): _____

Penalties: _____

Penalty Minutes: _____

Favorite Game Memory: _____
_____

Additional Game Notes/Stats:
_____
_____
_____
_____
_____
_____
_____
_____

Date: _____

Hockey League Level: _____

Location: _____

Team Name: _____

Opponent: _____

Position: _____

Shots Taken: _____ Goals: _____

Assists: _____ Power Play Goals: _____

Short Handed Goals: _____ Overtime Goals: _____

Game Winning Goal (Y/N): _____

Penalties: _____

Penalty Minutes: _____

Favorite Game Memory: _____

_____

Additional Game Notes/Stats:

_____

_____

_____

_____

_____

_____

_____

Date: _____

Hockey League Level: _____

Location: _____

Team Name: _____

Opponent: _____

Position: _____

Shots Taken: _____   Goals: _____

Assists: _____   Power Play Goals: _____

Short Handed Goals: _____   Overtime Goals: _____

Game Winning Goal (Y/N): _____

Penalties: _____

Penalty Minutes: _____

Favorite Game Memory: _____
_____

Additional Game Notes/Stats:
_____
_____
_____
_____
_____
_____
_____
_____
_____

Date: _____

Hockey League Level: _____

Location: _____

Team Name: _____

Opponent: _____

Position: _____

Shots Taken: _____   Goals: _____

Assists: _____   Power Play Goals: _____

Short Handed Goals: _____   Overtime Goals: _____

Game Winning Goal (Y/N): _____

Penalties: _____

Penalty Minutes: _____

Favorite Game Memory: _____
_____

Additional Game Notes/Stats:
_____
_____
_____
_____
_____
_____

Date: _____

Hockey League Level: _____

Location: _____

Team Name: _____

Opponent: _____

Position: _____

Shots Taken: _____ Goals: _____

Assists: _____ Power Play Goals: _____

Short Handed Goals: _____ Overtime Goals: _____

Game Winning Goal (Y/N): _____

Penalties: _____

Penalty Minutes: _____

Favorite Game Memory: _____

_____

Additional Game Notes/Stats:

_____
_____
_____
_____
_____
_____
_____
_____

Date: _____

Hockey League Level: _____

Location: _____

Team Name: _____

Opponent: _____

Position: _____

Shots Taken: _____ Goals: _____

Assists: _____ Power Play Goals: _____

Short Handed Goals: _____ Overtime Goals: _____

Game Winning Goal (Y/N): _____

Penalties: _____

Penalty Minutes: _____

Favorite Game Memory: _____
_____

Additional Game Notes/Stats:
_____
_____
_____
_____
_____
_____
_____

Date: _____

Hockey League Level: _____

Location: _____

Team Name: _____

Opponent: _____

Position: _____

Shots Taken: _____ Goals: _____

Assists: _____ Power Play Goals: _____

Short Handed Goals: _____ Overtime Goals: _____

Game Winning Goal (Y/N): _____

Penalties: _____

Penalty Minutes: _____

Favorite Game Memory: _____
_____

Additional Game Notes/Stats:
_____
_____
_____
_____
_____
_____
_____
_____

Date: _____

Hockey League Level: _____

Location: _____

Team Name: _____

Opponent: _____

Position: _____

Shots Taken: _____ Goals: _____

Assists: _____ Power Play Goals: _____

Short Handed Goals: _____ Overtime Goals: _____

Game Winning Goal (Y/N): _____

Penalties: _____

Penalty Minutes: _____

Favorite Game Memory: _____

_____

Additional Game Notes/Stats:

_____

_____

_____

_____

_____

_____

_____

Date: _____

Hockey League Level: _____

Location: _____

Team Name: _____

Opponent: _____

Position: _____

Shots Taken: _____ Goals: _____

Assists: _____ Power Play Goals: _____

Short Handed Goals: _____ Overtime Goals: _____

Game Winning Goal (Y/N): _____

Penalties: _____

Penalty Minutes: _____

Favorite Game Memory: _____

_____

Additional Game Notes/Stats:

_____

_____

_____

_____

_____

_____

_____

_____

Date: _____

Hockey League Level: _____

Location: _____

Team Name: _____

Opponent: _____

Position: _____

Shots Taken: _____   Goals: _____

Assists: _____   Power Play Goals: _____

Short Handed Goals: _____   Overtime Goals: _____

Game Winning Goal (Y/N): _____

Penalties: _____

Penalty Minutes: _____

Favorite Game Memory: _____

_____

Additional Game Notes/Stats:

_____

_____

_____

_____

_____

_____

_____

Date: _____

Hockey League Level: _____

Location: _____

Team Name: _____

Opponent: _____

Position: _____

Shots Taken: _____   Goals: _____

Assists: _____   Power Play Goals: _____

Short Handed Goals: _____   Overtime Goals: _____

Game Winning Goal (Y/N): _____

Penalties: _____

Penalty Minutes: _____

Favorite Game Memory: _____
_____

Additional Game Notes/Stats:
_____
_____
_____
_____
_____
_____
_____
_____
_____

Date: _____

Hockey League Level: _____

Location: _____

Team Name: _____

Opponent: _____

Position: _____

Shots Taken: _____   Goals: _____

Assists: _____   Power Play Goals: _____

Short Handed Goals: _____   Overtime Goals: _____

Game Winning Goal (Y/N): _____

Penalties: _____

Penalty Minutes: _____

Favorite Game Memory: _____

_____

Additional Game Notes/Stats:

_____

_____

_____

_____

_____

_____

_____

Date: _____

Hockey League Level: _____

Location: _____

Team Name: _____

Opponent: _____

Position: _____

Shots Taken: _____ Goals: _____

Assists: _____ Power Play Goals: _____

Short Handed Goals: _____ Overtime Goals: _____

Game Winning Goal (Y/N): _____

Penalties: _____

Penalty Minutes: _____

Favorite Game Memory: _____
_____

Additional Game Notes/Stats:
_____
_____
_____
_____
_____
_____
_____
_____
_____

Date: _____

Hockey League Level: _____

Location: _____

Team Name: _____

Opponent: _____

Position: _____

Shots Taken: _____   Goals: _____

Assists: _____   Power Play Goals: _____

Short Handed Goals: _____   Overtime Goals: _____

Game Winning Goal (Y/N): _____

Penalties: _____

Penalty Minutes: _____

Favorite Game Memory: _____
_____

Additional Game Notes/Stats:
_____
_____
_____
_____
_____
_____
_____
_____

Date: _____

Hockey League Level: _____

Location: _____

Team Name: _____

Opponent: _____

Position: _____

Shots Taken: _____ Goals: _____

Assists: _____ Power Play Goals: _____

Short Handed Goals: _____ Overtime Goals: _____

Game Winning Goal (Y/N): _____

Penalties: _____

Penalty Minutes: _____

Favorite Game Memory: _____
_____

Additional Game Notes/Stats:
_____
_____
_____
_____
_____
_____
_____
_____
_____
_____

Date: _____

Hockey League Level: _____

Location: _____

Team Name: _____

Opponent: _____

Position: _____

Shots Taken: _____ Goals: _____

Assists: _____ Power Play Goals: _____

Short Handed Goals: _____ Overtime Goals: _____

Game Winning Goal (Y/N): _____

Penalties: _____

Penalty Minutes: _____

Favorite Game Memory: _____

_____

Additional Game Notes/Stats:

_____

_____

_____

_____

_____

_____

_____

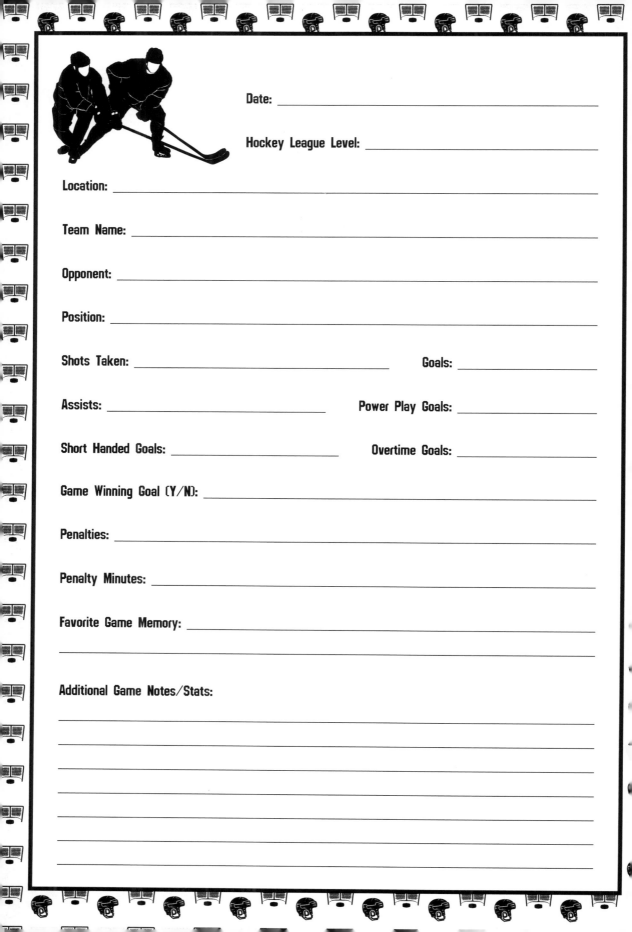

Date: _____

Hockey League Level: _____

Location: _____

Team Name: _____

Opponent: _____

Position: _____

Shots Taken: _____ Goals: _____

Assists: _____ Power Play Goals: _____

Short Handed Goals: _____ Overtime Goals: _____

Game Winning Goal (Y/N): _____

Penalties: _____

Penalty Minutes: _____

Favorite Game Memory: _____
_____

Additional Game Notes/Stats:
_____
_____
_____
_____
_____
_____
_____
_____
_____

Date: _____

Hockey League Level: _____

Location: _____

Team Name: _____

Opponent: _____

Position: _____

Shots Taken: _____   Goals: _____

Assists: _____   Power Play Goals: _____

Short Handed Goals: _____   Overtime Goals: _____

Game Winning Goal (Y/N): _____

Penalties: _____

Penalty Minutes: _____

Favorite Game Memory: _____
_____

Additional Game Notes/Stats:
_____
_____
_____
_____
_____
_____
_____
_____

Date: _____

Hockey League Level: _____

Location: _____

Team Name: _____

Opponent: _____

Position: _____

Shots Taken: _____   Goals: _____

Assists: _____   Power Play Goals: _____

Short Handed Goals: _____   Overtime Goals: _____

Game Winning Goal (Y/N): _____

Penalties: _____

Penalty Minutes: _____

Favorite Game Memory: _____
_____

Additional Game Notes/Stats:
_____
_____
_____
_____
_____
_____
_____
_____

Date: _____

Hockey League Level: _____

Location: _____

Team Name: _____

Opponent: _____

Position: _____

Shots Taken: _____ Goals: _____

Assists: _____ Power Play Goals: _____

Short Handed Goals: _____ Overtime Goals: _____

Game Winning Goal (Y/N): _____

Penalties: _____

Penalty Minutes: _____

Favorite Game Memory: _____
_____

Additional Game Notes/Stats:
_____
_____
_____
_____
_____
_____
_____

Date: _____

Hockey League Level: _____

Location: _____

Team Name: _____

Opponent: _____

Position: _____

Shots Taken: _____ Goals: _____

Assists: _____ Power Play Goals: _____

Short Handed Goals: _____ Overtime Goals: _____

Game Winning Goal (Y/N): _____

Penalties: _____

Penalty Minutes: _____

Favorite Game Memory: _____
_____

Additional Game Notes/Stats:
_____
_____
_____
_____
_____
_____
_____
_____
_____

Date: _____

Hockey League Level: _____

Location: _____

Team Name: _____

Opponent: _____

Position: _____

Shots Taken: _____   Goals: _____

Assists: _____   Power Play Goals: _____

Short Handed Goals: _____   Overtime Goals: _____

Game Winning Goal (Y/N): _____

Penalties: _____

Penalty Minutes: _____

Favorite Game Memory: _____
_____

Additional Game Notes/Stats:
_____
_____
_____
_____
_____
_____
_____

Date: _____

Hockey League Level: _____

Location: _____

Team Name: _____

Opponent: _____

Position: _____

Shots Taken: _____ Goals: _____

Assists: _____ Power Play Goals: _____

Short Handed Goals: _____ Overtime Goals: _____

Game Winning Goal (Y/N): _____

Penalties: _____

Penalty Minutes: _____

Favorite Game Memory: _____
_____

Additional Game Notes/Stats:
_____
_____
_____
_____
_____
_____
_____
_____

Date: _____

Hockey League Level: _____

Location: _____

Team Name: _____

Opponent: _____

Position: _____

Shots Taken: _____   Goals: _____

Assists: _____   Power Play Goals: _____

Short Handed Goals: _____   Overtime Goals: _____

Game Winning Goal (Y/N): _____

Penalties: _____

Penalty Minutes: _____

Favorite Game Memory: _____

_____

Additional Game Notes/Stats:

_____

_____

_____

_____

_____

_____

_____

Date: _____

Hockey League Level: _____

Location: _____

Team Name: _____

Opponent: _____

Position: _____

Shots Taken: _____   Goals: _____

Assists: _____   Power Play Goals: _____

Short Handed Goals: _____   Overtime Goals: _____

Game Winning Goal (Y/N): _____

Penalties: _____

Penalty Minutes: _____

Favorite Game Memory: _____
_____

Additional Game Notes/Stats:
_____
_____
_____
_____
_____
_____
_____
_____
_____

Date: _____

Hockey League Level: _____

Location: _____

Team Name: _____

Opponent: _____

Position: _____

Shots Taken: _____   Goals: _____

Assists: _____   Power Play Goals: _____

Short Handed Goals: _____   Overtime Goals: _____

Game Winning Goal (Y/N): _____

Penalties: _____

Penalty Minutes: _____

Favorite Game Memory: _____

_____

Additional Game Notes/Stats:

_____

_____

_____

_____

_____

_____

_____

Date: _____

Hockey League Level: _____

Location: _____

Team Name: _____

Opponent: _____

Position: _____

Shots Taken: _____ Goals: _____

Assists: _____ Power Play Goals: _____

Short Handed Goals: _____ Overtime Goals: _____

Game Winning Goal (Y/N): _____

Penalties: _____

Penalty Minutes: _____

Favorite Game Memory: _____

_____

Additional Game Notes/Stats:

_____

_____

_____

_____

_____

_____

_____

_____

_____

Date: _____

Hockey League Level: _____

Location: _____

Team Name: _____

Opponent: _____

Position: _____

Shots Taken: _____   Goals: _____

Assists: _____   Power Play Goals: _____

Short Handed Goals: _____   Overtime Goals: _____

Game Winning Goal (Y/N): _____

Penalties: _____

Penalty Minutes: _____

Favorite Game Memory: _____
_____

Additional Game Notes/Stats:
_____
_____
_____
_____
_____
_____
_____

Date: _____

Hockey League Level: _____

Location: _____

Team Name: _____

Opponent: _____

Position: _____

Shots Taken: _____   Goals: _____

Assists: _____   Power Play Goals: _____

Short Handed Goals: _____   Overtime Goals: _____

Game Winning Goal (Y/N): _____

Penalties: _____

Penalty Minutes: _____

Favorite Game Memory: _____

_____

Additional Game Notes/Stats:

_____

_____

_____

_____

_____

_____

_____

_____

_____

Date: _____

Hockey League Level: _____

Location: _____

Team Name: _____

Opponent: _____

Position: _____

Shots Taken: _____   Goals: _____

Assists: _____   Power Play Goals: _____

Short Handed Goals: _____   Overtime Goals: _____

Game Winning Goal (Y/N): _____

Penalties: _____

Penalty Minutes: _____

Favorite Game Memory: _____

_____

Additional Game Notes/Stats:

_____
_____
_____
_____
_____
_____
_____
_____

Date: _____

Hockey League Level: _____

Location: _____

Team Name: _____

Opponent: _____

Position: _____

Shots Taken: _____   Goals: _____

Assists: _____   Power Play Goals: _____

Short Handed Goals: _____   Overtime Goals: _____

Game Winning Goal (Y/N): _____

Penalties: _____

Penalty Minutes: _____

Favorite Game Memory: _____
_____

Additional Game Notes/Stats:
_____
_____
_____
_____
_____
_____
_____
_____

Date: _____

Hockey League Level: _____

Location: _____

Team Name: _____

Opponent: _____

Position: _____

Shots Taken: _____ Goals: _____

Assists: _____ Power Play Goals: _____

Short Handed Goals: _____ Overtime Goals: _____

Game Winning Goal (Y/N): _____

Penalties: _____

Penalty Minutes: _____

Favorite Game Memory: _____
_____

Additional Game Notes/Stats:
_____
_____
_____
_____
_____
_____
_____
_____

Date: _____

Hockey League Level: _____

Location: _____

Team Name: _____

Opponent: _____

Position: _____

Shots Taken: _____ **Goals:** _____

Assists: _____ **Power Play Goals:** _____

Short Handed Goals: _____ **Overtime Goals:** _____

Game Winning Goal (Y/N): _____

Penalties: _____

Penalty Minutes: _____

Favorite Game Memory: _____
_____

Additional Game Notes/Stats:
_____
_____
_____
_____
_____
_____
_____
_____
_____

Date: _____

Hockey League Level: _____

Location: _____

Team Name: _____

Opponent: _____

Position: _____

Shots Taken: _____   Goals: _____

Assists: _____   Power Play Goals: _____

Short Handed Goals: _____   Overtime Goals: _____

Game Winning Goal (Y/N): _____

Penalties: _____

Penalty Minutes: _____

Favorite Game Memory: _____

_____

Additional Game Notes/Stats:

_____

_____

_____

_____

_____

_____

_____

_____

Date: _____

Hockey League Level: _____

Location: _____

Team Name: _____

Opponent: _____

Position: _____

Shots Taken: _____ Goals: _____

Assists: _____ Power Play Goals: _____

Short Handed Goals: _____ Overtime Goals: _____

Game Winning Goal (Y/N): _____

Penalties: _____

Penalty Minutes: _____

Favorite Game Memory: _____
_____

Additional Game Notes/Stats:
_____
_____
_____
_____
_____
_____
_____
_____
_____

Date: _____

Hockey League Level: _____

Location: _____

Team Name: _____

Opponent: _____

Position: _____

Shots Taken: _____ Goals: _____

Assists: _____ Power Play Goals: _____

Short Handed Goals: _____ Overtime Goals: _____

Game Winning Goal (Y/N): _____

Penalties: _____

Penalty Minutes: _____

Favorite Game Memory: _____
_____

Additional Game Notes/Stats:
_____
_____
_____
_____
_____
_____
_____
_____

Date: _____

Hockey League Level: _____

Location: _____

Team Name: _____

Opponent: _____

Position: _____

Shots Taken: _____ Goals: _____

Assists: _____ Power Play Goals: _____

Short Handed Goals: _____ Overtime Goals: _____

Game Winning Goal (Y/N): _____

Penalties: _____

Penalty Minutes: _____

Favorite Game Memory: _____
_____

Additional Game Notes/Stats:
_____
_____
_____
_____
_____
_____
_____
_____
_____

Date: _____

Hockey League Level: _____

Location: _____

Team Name: _____

Opponent: _____

Position: _____

Shots Taken: _____   Goals: _____

Assists: _____   Power Play Goals: _____

Short Handed Goals: _____   Overtime Goals: _____

Game Winning Goal (Y/N): _____

Penalties: _____

Penalty Minutes: _____

Favorite Game Memory: _____
_____

Additional Game Notes/Stats:

_____
_____
_____
_____
_____
_____
_____

Date: _____

Hockey League Level: _____

Location: _____

Team Name: _____

Opponent: _____

Position: _____

Shots Taken: _____ Goals: _____

Assists: _____ Power Play Goals: _____

Short Handed Goals: _____ Overtime Goals: _____

Game Winning Goal (Y/N): _____

Penalties: _____

Penalty Minutes: _____

Favorite Game Memory: _____

_____

Additional Game Notes/Stats:

_____

_____

_____

_____

_____

_____

_____

_____

Date: _____

Hockey League Level: _____

Location: _____

Team Name: _____

Opponent: _____

Position: _____

Shots Taken: _____ Goals: _____

Assists: _____ Power Play Goals: _____

Short Handed Goals: _____ Overtime Goals: _____

Game Winning Goal (Y/N): _____

Penalties: _____

Penalty Minutes: _____

Favorite Game Memory: _____

_____

Additional Game Notes/Stats:

_____

_____

_____

_____

_____

_____

_____

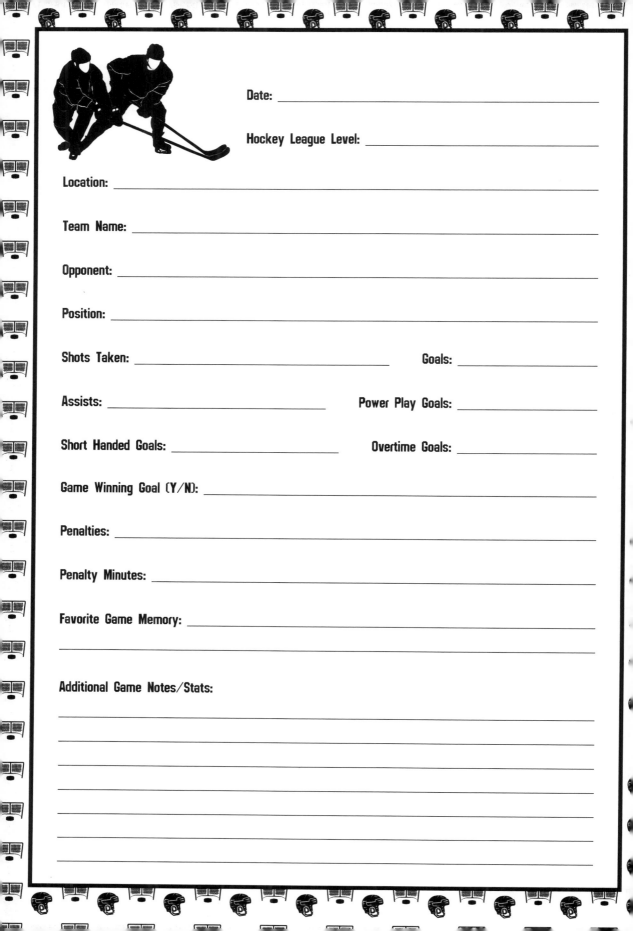

Date: _____

Hockey League Level: _____

Location: _____

Team Name: _____

Opponent: _____

Position: _____

Shots Taken: _____   Goals: _____

Assists: _____   Power Play Goals: _____

Short Handed Goals: _____   Overtime Goals: _____

Game Winning Goal (Y/N): _____

Penalties: _____

Penalty Minutes: _____

Favorite Game Memory: _____
_____

Additional Game Notes/Stats:
_____
_____
_____
_____
_____
_____
_____
_____
_____

Date: _____

Hockey League Level: _____

Location: _____

Team Name: _____

Opponent: _____

Position: _____

Shots Taken: _____   Goals: _____

Assists: _____   Power Play Goals: _____

Short Handed Goals: _____   Overtime Goals: _____

Game Winning Goal (Y/N): _____

Penalties: _____

Penalty Minutes: _____

Favorite Game Memory: _____
_____

Additional Game Notes/Stats:
_____
_____
_____
_____
_____
_____
_____
_____

Date: _____

Hockey League Level: _____

Location: _____

Team Name: _____

Opponent: _____

Position: _____

Shots Taken: _____ Goals: _____

Assists: _____ Power Play Goals: _____

Short Handed Goals: _____ Overtime Goals: _____

Game Winning Goal (Y/N): _____

Penalties: _____

Penalty Minutes: _____

Favorite Game Memory: _____

_____

Additional Game Notes/Stats:

_____
_____
_____
_____
_____
_____
_____
_____
_____

Date: _____

Hockey League Level: _____

Location: _____

Team Name: _____

Opponent: _____

Position: _____

Shots Taken: _____ Goals: _____

Assists: _____ Power Play Goals: _____

Short Handed Goals: _____ Overtime Goals: _____

Game Winning Goal (Y/N): _____

Penalties: _____

Penalty Minutes: _____

Favorite Game Memory: _____

_____

Additional Game Notes/Stats:

_____
_____
_____
_____
_____
_____
_____
_____

Date: _____

Hockey League Level: _____

Location: _____

Team Name: _____

Opponent: _____

Position: _____

Shots Taken: _____   Goals: _____

Assists: _____   Power Play Goals: _____

Short Handed Goals: _____   Overtime Goals: _____

Game Winning Goal (Y/N): _____

Penalties: _____

Penalty Minutes: _____

Favorite Game Memory: _____
_____

Additional Game Notes/Stats:
_____
_____
_____
_____
_____
_____
_____
_____
_____

Date: _____

Hockey League Level: _____

Location: _____

Team Name: _____

Opponent: _____

Position: _____

Shots Taken: _____ Goals: _____

Assists: _____ Power Play Goals: _____

Short Handed Goals: _____ Overtime Goals: _____

Game Winning Goal (Y/N): _____

Penalties: _____

Penalty Minutes: _____

Favorite Game Memory: _____

_____

Additional Game Notes/Stats:

_____
_____
_____
_____
_____
_____
_____

Date: _____

Hockey League Level: _____

Location: _____

Team Name: _____

Opponent: _____

Position: _____

Shots Taken: _____   Goals: _____

Assists: _____   Power Play Goals: _____

Short Handed Goals: _____   Overtime Goals: _____

Game Winning Goal (Y/N): _____

Penalties: _____

Penalty Minutes: _____

Favorite Game Memory: _____
_____

Additional Game Notes/Stats:
_____
_____
_____
_____
_____
_____
_____
_____
_____

Date: _____

Hockey League Level: _____

Location: _____

Team Name: _____

Opponent: _____

Position: _____

Shots Taken: _____   Goals: _____

Assists: _____   Power Play Goals: _____

Short Handed Goals: _____   Overtime Goals: _____

Game Winning Goal (Y/N): _____

Penalties: _____

Penalty Minutes: _____

Favorite Game Memory: _____

_____

Additional Game Notes/Stats:

_____
_____
_____
_____
_____
_____
_____

Date: _____

Hockey League Level: _____

Location: _____

Team Name: _____

Opponent: _____

Position: _____

Shots Taken: _____ Goals: _____

Assists: _____ Power Play Goals: _____

Short Handed Goals: _____ Overtime Goals: _____

Game Winning Goal (Y/N): _____

Penalties: _____

Penalty Minutes: _____

Favorite Game Memory: _____

_____

Additional Game Notes/Stats:

_____

_____

_____

_____

_____

_____

_____

_____

_____

Made in the USA
Columbia, SC
27 May 2017